Poiesis
REVIEW

ISSUES ONE
through
FIVE

Violet Ray
SERIES

ISSUES ONE *through* FIVE

Various Authors

Curated and Edited by
Leah Angstman

Alternating Current Press
Boulder, Colorado

LETTER

This archival collection may require a little more explanation than most journals do. *Poiesis Review* is a remnant of my teenage years, making cut 'n' paste zines and chapbooks in my bedroom, writing out pages by hand before dot-matrix printers and dial-up connections made my life easier (yet, somehow more complicated), hand-collating and -stapling, licking shut hundreds of envelopes per issue. Some of the poems in this collection even predate the humble little press I started back in 1993, acquired in those early days from stacks of poems that poets circulated on typewriter carbon paper for years before landing a space on some page. The game was different.

And the world was different. With the earliest poem in here dating back to 1991 and the latest poem dating to 2012, there is a lot of ground covered here, but it's also pre-Trumpian ground. The tone is decidedly different from poems and journals we see today. The urgency is softer. The pace is not so frantic. It has the archival smell of a place and time that existed long before the dumpster fire of the year in which this compilation is being printed. In the midst of a global pandemic, an authoritarian presidential administration, unchecked police violence, the Me Too movement, and a Second Civil Rights Era erupting for justice and equality across the nation, it's odd to read words about things that are so markedly in the past. Tupac. Obama. George W. Bush. September 11th. Wayne Gretsky. AIDS. Jack Micheline. Hope.

The writing is quieter and has that leftover Beat feel to it, so much of it being written by 1990s and early aughts staples who were as much a remnant of their post-Beat generations as I am now an obvious child of that forgotten generation that fell between Gen X and the millennials. Many of the authors have passed away, and still more have been lost to me through the years of changed mailing addresses, email bouncebacks, and occupation shifts that actually bring a paycheck.

But the words and the time are important, and not just sentimentally. We strive to document history, to keep the words of our past alive, and so many of those words have been rescued throughout history by "the little guys"—the small presses and underdog presses and oddity presses and diversity presses that have captured entire eras and ages from the shallow depths of their own pockets. This press started out "for the love of it," and though it's entered the commercial world, the writing is still loved, always, first and foremost, loved, loved. And things that are loved should be preserved, so that when the world finally falls all the way apart, and we're forced to rebuild from what little remains, these words will still be here to tell the new world the most personal thing a poet will tell you: *I existed. We existed. We gave you our words, and they outlived us.*

There are notes I should mention about this collection before I leave you to it. *Poiesis Review* started as a poetry journal. Issues no. 1-5, collected here, are all poetry. Beginning with issue no. 6 in 2013, fiction and nonfiction came into play, and that changed the whole direction of our press, which had primarily feasted on poetry until then. I should mention, as well, to avoid confusion, that some poems have been removed from this anthology to be better placed elsewhere, in other collections of older chapbooks we're newly compiling for the Violet Ray Series. In order to publish two decades' worth of archives effectively, we're grouping authors together according to style and volume of work; if a piece is missing from this repertoire that you remembered being here, it's been moved elsewhere for a better fit.

Contained within are poems from as far back as 1991, and up to 2012. In this span of time (and since), we lost some of our own along the way. This collection is dedicated to the memories of those poets who entrusted Alternating Current with keeping their words alive, for generations to come.

Jack Micheline
1929-1998

Giovanni Malito
passed on October 19, 2003

Hayden Carruth
1921-2008

Tim Scannell
passed in November 2010

Aleksey Dayen
passed on November 20, 2010

Joe Speer
passed on January 25, 2011

Arthur Winfield Knight
December 29, 1937-September 7, 2012

Robert Schuler
1939-September 15, 2018

don't use the telephone
people are never ready to answer it
use poetry
                    —Jack Kerouac

TABLE OF CONTENTS

POETRY

NO. 5 — 2012

LUMINAIRE POETRY AWARD WINNERS

Poiesis

REVIEW
ISSUE ONE

IN THE POETRY SECTION OF BROWN UNIVERSITY BOOKSTORE, PROVIDENCE, RI

ZOE A. JAIMOT

When you ask me where are the poets of today—

I can answer you emphatically
that I have seen them skulking
among empty spaces full of pages—

When you ask me where are these modern versifiers—

I can tell you that I have seen them
continually among a fog of books—

And I have seen these geniuses of writing classes
haphazardly thumb through volumes
while they sit among smashed verbs—
that go nowhere on shelves
inscribed and perfect-bound
with words that would be
wishing wells for these thick talkers—
for these borrowers of sentiment—

For these poets who carefully
coif and spike their outer anonymity
with streaks of purple angst—
looking like rock stars drugged
by just the proper dactyls
of urban trendiness while
these same self-proclaimed new-age poets
circle endlessly in apparent boredom—
like vultures eying these aisles to swoop
on those unsuspecting few—

14

who stop unaware
of this purposely planned introduction
to the "rap" and "spin" of modern verse—

Today's poets spring silently at their prey—
on boots better made for stomping than alliteration—
and casually pluck their own books from the racks—
and smile with a look of practiced sincerity—
while turning to say, "This person's pretty good"—
and then ask, "Have you read anything by them?"—
"You really should, you know," they say
with just a tinge of hipster/peer pressure in their tone—
"Everyone says it's better than an orgasm," they add
hoping to lure you with visions of quick sex—
always remembering to look deeply
as they speak false phrases—
hoping by the guile of personality
to achieve an apotheosis—
they could never reach by words
better left honestly alone—

WHITE BUTT BUDDHA

K. NUZZO

White butt Buddha
Open up to blue peace
Narrow path of third
Eye temple.

Sing flying blind crow
Sutra to disintegrate
Your caged scream
Prayer shift to
Blow holy trumpet
Of shining new
Life freedom chorus.

May the angels sing
Loudly where the
Highway of surrender
Gives out.

MOVING

ASHLEY GATEWOOD

New Jersey to New York to Arizona back to New Jersey
To California to Philadelphia to Pittsburgh.
I followed you around the country.
I stayed in your HoJos and climbed your Red Rocks.
I canceled two tickets: one plane and one bus.
To see you.
To see you.
It bled both of us into dehydration.
She's been standing inside of you since California,
Slowly edging me out,
Uprooting my concreted roots in you.
I turned my back for five days in Montreal and she took over.
Completely transferred me, out of a little town called Ocean City.

Maybe I never had a claim on as much of you as I thought.
Maybe she showed you the way to the King,
But did she ever teach you to use your wings?

VOID—TIME WINERY

Mercedes hates having purplish people
whizzing on her grapes
"they'll have %&#@$ trouble
becoming wine" she laments ...
but sorrytosay, so-exposed arbor vines
pose just too much
of a temptation nowadays—
and the rain, well, it's trying its
deluging best to keep up
but finally defers to the simple snow
so gently fag-falling
flakes attaching their burrs
onto the clusters & bunches &
broadgreen leaves ... being nature's
most gentle purifying flush

THE INDEPENDENCE OF DECLARATION

R. EMOLO

Anything electrical can seduce
And blind you—the TV, the Internet.
Some of our best and brightest are selling us out.
They've succumbed to something as ignorant as ignorance.
Because I'm an artist, I'm made to feel like a persecuted Jew
Before the Second World War.
They're phasing us out, the middle class on down.
To secede from the Union is a coward's way of saying traitor.
There is no national debt; this country doesn't owe the devil a dime.
They warned us about communism,
Yet they use fascism to protect democracy.
You do your best to be a caring American,
And they treat you as if you were a social disease.
To care is worth caring about.

SADLY, IN PATTER RAIN MATTERS

DAN BUCK

Life quickly dies down
from its worried speed,
moving time over, clear through,
to, till the start
of the beginning in its dead lies
that lay in, down over truth,
wearing me slowly, more nervous.

DEEP IS AN OCEAN

GIOVANNI MALITO

you are a puddle
and raindrops
        are bombs

breathe, breathe air
water contains oxygen
but you need air

raise your head
raise it through clouds—
you won't puncture
        the ozone layer

look around,
the sky is blue
but each raindrop
has no hue, colorless

as was your puddle
before the silt gathered
        to make mud

the ocean is blue
but the ocean is deep

        it can swallow
a puddle like you

                if you let it

JESUS SAVES

PATRICK MCKINNON

gretsky
in the crease!

gets the rebound!

he shoots
he scores!

POETRY IN AMERICA

MICHAEL KRIESEL

People washing dishes
publish poems
a hundred see

riding 20 hours
on a bus
to see each other

drunk
on 3rd shift

see their kids
on weekends

given time
the best might
never write another line

CONTEMPORARY ART LEFTOVERS

P. B. C.

Video as film
Lacking substance
Dumbass performance
Finding warehouse space

Institution insularity
Based on self-interest
Not even
A 2-day symposium

Theater of the empire
On East Houston Street
Fueled by sales
Of used cars

Modern art—d'art moderne
Panhandles current painting
And our new sculpture
Concrete parentheses

JUMPER

KEVIN M. HIBSHMAN

sorrow in the face
of the wafer-thin girl.
child-bone borne through the
heart and arteries of bedlam to
be suspended in deathless flight.
she got the world figured out,
all right.

DO I KNOW YOU?

NEAL WILGUS

an old friend I'd never met
was waiting in the kitchen
saying come on in make it home
let's kick back enjoy
a familiar voice I knew
was not one I knew
not one I recognized
as someone I'd done things
with when we were young
we hadn't stayed up
most of the night
talking about everything
and nothing at all
hadn't wandered the streets
together or driven in fear
to hide from the cops
hadn't been dead drunk
together or staggered around
looking for something to smoke
hadn't agreed to disagree
and finally seen things
so differently that we
might not be speaking
the same tongue
no this guy was someone
whom I should have known
all these years
but somehow he'd been
somewhere else all the time
or I'd been out of town
which was the same thing
but old friends or new friends
friends are friends
so I sat and we had a drink
together

VANISHING HURRICANE IS A SONG

WILLIAM MARTINEZ

to sing into dark winds or the
crush of night
poetry. evidence. epic-prayer.
[confession—observation]
These are my diaries,
brief & sparse
of love & suffering
too profound to narrate.

The simultaneous contraction &
explosion of my time [history, future, present]
overwhelms
an intimate tide
   pulled in—stretched back
by a paradox moon.
My nobody selfhood, a thousand subtle bodies
moving together in one body.

In the end after our
last breath has parted
we find
nothing
at all
to say

but "on the breath" takes practice
[lifelong affirming until we stop breathing]
   Breath "the world gives off in swirling waves"
of golden-ebony full spectrum
light—beyond—light
In infinite-part harmony
No thing to hold on to
No thing to give up
So very much to pass through
      pass back   pass away

NON PUGNALATE LA PACE

FERRUCCIO BRUGNARO

Non divorate la pace.
Non rispondete alle montagne
                    di morti
            con altre montagne
                        di morti.
Spegnete la fame nello sguardo
                di milioni
                    di bambini.

        Accendete
        il sorriso
        sulla terra di Palestina
        accendete il canto.
Non pugnalate
            non pugnalate la pace
                    alle spalle.
Togliete il cappio di solitudine
            al popolo irakeno
                al popolo cubano.
Abbattete la notte agghiacciante
                        profonda
            in cui vagano
        milioni di creature.
Non rispondete
            non rispondete
                    ai morti
        con infiniti roghi
                di altre vite.
Mordetevi le labbra forte
            mordetevi forte il cuore.
        Non inneggiate alla guerra.
        Non inneggiate alla guerra.

DON'T STAB PEACE

FERRUCCIO BRUGNARO

Translated from the Italian by JACK HIRSCHMAN

Don't devour peace
Don't respond to the mountains
                    of dead people
            with more mountains
                        of dead.
Put out the hunger in the look
                of millions
                        of kids.
        Kindle
        the smile
        on the land of Palestine
        light the song.
Don't stab
Don't stab peace
            in the back.
Remove the noose of loneliness
            from the Iraqi people
                from the Cuban people.
Break down the freezing
                    deep night
            millions of creatures wander in.
Don't respond,
        don't respond to the dead
            with infinite pyres of other lives.
Bite your lips hard down,
            bite your heart hard.
        Don't exalt war.
        Don't exalt war.

CRACKER'S BABY

SHERRY ASBURY

Everyone calls her Cracker.
She's 14 years old ... almost.
She is the queen of the park,
goes with anyone who pays.
A baby grows within her now.
Where it came from—
she doesn't know or care.
She wishes it were gone.
Barbie dolls and virginal
innocence should fill
the fabric of her days,
but Mom's new man liked
little girls.
Cracker ran away when
he raped her and her mother
pretended not to know.
Life taught her that her
womanhood is a commodity—
sold to the highest bidder.
Uptown white lady
steps around Cracker's cortège
of eager young men,
waiting for their turn.
Woman ignores the girl's
proffered palm with a rude push.
"I don't pay for you to play,"
says this upstanding citizen
with a sniff.
Inside the coffeeshop
the woman runs her hand
lovingly over several
cappuccino machines.
Puts one on the gold card.

CLEANING UP AT THE HAMTRAMCK BURGER CHEF

DON WINTER

Nights at this place
boss lines spray bottles up
across the counter. He says the red's
for shelves, the blue's for toilets,
and the white's only for stainless steel.
His eyebrows frown, but when
that bastard disappears into his office
I spray what I want
onto what I want.

Some nights his wife lifts
her ass onto the counter. She points
out turnover skins I missed.
Looks like she's been slept in
for years. Those nights I time
his trip to the bank so I can chase
her with the white bottle.
I catch her and squeeze
the little Chef faces stitched
over her breasts.

But most nights the boss
looks right through me. His wife cleans
the salad bar, and yells
at the bits of mustard and dressing.
As if they were to blame
for all this. One night boss yelled
What are you sittin' around for?
Go home and get yourself
a piece of ass. I turned to him.
I am a piece of ass.
He laughed at that
so I said it louder.

Poiesis
REVIEW
ISSUE TWO

THE ROSEBUD

JASON FISK

I hadn't seen you
since the day you told
me you were pregnant,
in that café. It was
a September day,
filled with a cold fall rain.
I remember thinking
that I could smell the rain
on people as they passed us.
There was an unopened
rosebud in a simple
glass vase on our table.
"What am I going to do?"
you asked
over and over.

Today we stood in the aisle
between the cards
and the candles
at Target, small talk
our armor. I looked
at your empty belly.
You pulled your jacket closed.
"Well, it sure is good to see you.
We'll have to get together sometime,"
you lied. I wanted to tell you
that I had learned
in a poem
that the Japanese
prefer the rose bud
to the rose blossom,
but how to fit that
into conversation?

AND THEN AGAIN

FATHER LUKE

there are moments
in each day when it all just seems to
make sense

there is a comfort in that
a repose from all the troubles
of an entire lifetime

those moments don't last very long at all,
and then the confusion begins again

moments of clarity are highly overrated,
but unfortunately they are unavoidable

A MOTHER'S MANTRA

REBECCA SCHUMEJDA

for Liz Graziano

To hell with the dishes, the dust,
the dirt, the diapers, the drudgeries.

I sweep crumbs under carpets,
toss toys haphazardly out of view,
sniff test the laundry to lighten the load
while dragging my teething daughter
behind me like a soapy mop.

I know I shouldn't envy the man
who needs not abandon thought
to attend his crying infant, or ailing household;
who does not have to microwave his coffee
three times before taking one sip;
whose wardrobe is not Jackson Pollock-ed
with a colorful assortment of baby food.

But I do.

To hell with the dishes, the dust,
the dirt, the diapers, the drudgeries.

Last Easter eve, with my daughter
somersaulting inside me,
like a Tibetan prayer flag releasing its mantra,
I tried to persuade a veteran mother
that our art does not have to suffer
because we are women.
Thank you for allowing me
to remain disillusioned
for the last few months
of my pregnancy.

THE FALL OF MISS SOPA, EATER OF CLAY

JULIE BUFFALOE-YODER

Sopa Abraham Botswana Jonson, b. 1907

Before three men and ten babies
parted her legs with a prayer,
Miss Sopa danced at the shore
with the women of time,
the women who ate clay
and kneeled naked
in autumn water at dawn.

She danced to the beat
of the beacon, bright
in her bones, then gone.
She danced a celebration
of Someday; she danced
in the breath of the water,
water the breath for all men.

Makers of clay, eaters of clay,
morphine for the women—
blue-gray and smooth,
cool through her teeth.
Her stomach filled with clay.
She sang for breath
in spite of clay in her throat.

Men came and babies came.
Only the babies stayed
to bite the ends
of her night-numb breasts.
Only a scar remained
on her sweet dark cheek,
shaped like an open mouth
full of fat, white teeth.

She lived in a shack
held together by shadows,
and filled the holes
in her walls with clay.

Clay that cracked
and crumpled on the floor.
Clay swept outside
by a pinestraw broom.
Clay-gummed babies
(eight were all she had left).

One got caught
in a chicken-wire fence.
One lost an eye
on Good Friday.
One lost her foot
in a Goodwill shoe
when an ax dropped
from a large, hard hand.

Summers, she worked in quiet dirt,
through shimmers of heat, each year
a baby strapped to her back, rocked
to sleep by the bending; her songs
captured in straw baskets rustled
tobacco leaves like hungry birds.

She taught her daughters
how to walk tall
in thick-skinned mud
where she learned to crawl.

One by one her babies left.
One by one they came back
like cats, proud of the clay
they held in their mouths
but not enough teats
to go around.

Stretchmarks of red spread
across the setting sky
that last fall when Miss Sopa
led the women, hand in hand,
clothed in skin, three miles
to the Promised Shore
beyond sun-dotted woods.

They covered their tongues
with a thunderstorm of mud.
In a crash of tambourines,
they washed away the blood
beside a leaf-wet, fallen pine.

A shrine for the sinners,
the makers of clay.

FAIRYTALE

NEAL WILGUS

When the ship of sleep docked on my pillow, I was surprised at how small it was—surprised also that Captain Hook was in charge. The ship, he explained, could be whatever size I wanted, and he was only filling in for the regular guy.

A lot of people preferred SUVs, he said, and the regular guy was Rush Limbaugh. How come I didn't know anything about all this? I questioned, struggling to take in what he said. It's a pain in the ass, he sighed. We have to explain the whole damn thing over again every night.

MOSHE

JANICE BRABAW

You were too young to love me
The way I thought I needed to be loved
And in the end I wasn't enough
Too much
For you

I was too young to love you
The way you thought you needed to be loved
And in the end you weren't enough
Too much
For me

Dusk does not settle
Without the dust
Of our love
Whispering across
Floorboards
From under the door.

And every night
Before I sleep
I have to sweep it back
So I can rest again.

SECOND COMING

MICHAEL KRIESEL

Maybe
he'll come down
from all those
plaster crosses
all at once

ten thousand holy terrorists
taking on the government
like wish fulfillment

maybe
this time
he won't go away
maybe he'll turn
all the TVs off forever
and we'll have to talk

maybe
wake up naked
all of us with nothing
and we'll have to be

maybe
we're all dreaming
he's not coming
and it's time
to wake up hard as hell

and finish what he started

THE COMMISSAR OF BLOOMINGDALE'S

ZOE A. JAIMOT

He always espoused
the "leftist workers line"
Wearing his gold lamé turtleneck
Power to the people
Down with capitalism
Reciting the exact chorus
of every Broadway musical
including Kate Hepburn's
brief gig as "CoCo"
Admonishing those who dared
refer to anyone as divine except
the divine Maria Callas darling
As he fucked his way
through half of NYC
He'd done his master's thesis
on modern sexual behavior of course
Spending his life teaching at universities
Never getting tenure but cultivating
a wicked van-dyke to accompany
classic movie star looks akin
to an aging Tyrone Power or Ronald Coleman
Playing the role to the hilt
Always sitting outside a brasserie
Making sure he was seen
Making sure his Marxist-Leninist rant
was heard above the city's din
Telling me with sly titillation
leaning close as if this personal gossip
came from the CIA's secret vault
How the gallon size of Crisco
was so much more economical
for all his jabbings and thrustings
How it was organic and natural
And besides he stored it under
his tête-à-tête sofa so the red/white/blue

of the tin can wouldn't clash
After all he did have the most
egalitarian bedroom ensemble
Which did indeed welcome anyone
to experience his progressive philosophy
Doing away with "girlie" pinup calendars
and pictures of dead white male presidents

And when I found out about the virus
And that he would not be spared
He told me the only thing he ever wanted
was that after the revolution—
He wanted to be Commissar of Bloomingdale's
Running things for the good of the masses
Because style is never out of fashion
No matter what the political system.

LORD AND THE

ROD NAQUIN

fuckin debauchery, i was on
the sofa learning something about
physics and this dude was in
a chair. i got gas, burritos, just
twenty dollars and the car
wiggles. its familiar, like my glasses
or the clipse, something on
102.9. the dudes dad had curly
hair and this other girl wrote a
play, a play on words. somebody
went to jail, oops, do, wop,
oo, chalk. skulls i remember you,
sometimes you stick to the
sofa, she said. i was sweating,
laughed, fucked and cried.
thats what it sounded like.
or on a roof, tupac, two packs,
he wont smoke mine, fell off
the chair and the czech guy was
visiting me, he loved me, i loved
the dark beer, the light beer,
the light, lighting, lighter, her
and it all without a filter. or
was there one, goggles, im not
sure my voice is debauched. i
could hear it cracking, we
were stomping, restoring virginity,
the girls were worried, im not
sure. the lord and the reverend,
infomercials and then a football
game. the tires are flat,
where is the gas, im not sure.

JUNE

PAMELA ANNAS

Time for honeybees to travel
from clover to purple clover
to palimpsest white throats
of lilies, tracing secrets,
slipping inside pliant petals
to fly fat thighs of yellow dust
suitcases of pollen
past buttercups and pale
seed pods of weedy grass
preening as they pass
Boston/New York commuters
admiring their faces in the glass,
the dandelions' flat yellow mirrors.

ACCORDING TO ARISTOTLE

JASON MONIOS

Aristotle said that philosophy is not an art for young men,
but then he had not Socrates' interest in sodomy.

I beg to differ, on the question of age.
Philosophy is indeed for young men, and young men only.
That is when it matters that things should be thus and so,
that we felt the necessity, the need to know.
We could not bear to live without examination—

but now who needs it? Do I need to know the secrets
of the world, scan its depths? Can it make a difference to my action?
Would I not rather palm my head along the lengths
of rowdy concrete life, than give myself back to abstraction?

No, Aristotle got it wrong.

Philosophy is for the young, the young who strive and need.
The old know what is important, the little things that escape
the attention of philosophers. The correct weave for a pair of socks,
the right cut for a pair of trousers, the seasoning for a soup.

Here are the cataclysmic reactions,
giving the energy that sustains our world.
Here is your Big Bang, here your molecular masonry.
Big things are made of little things, and I marvel in the mundane.

WHY I GAVE UP WRITING AND JOINED THE CIRCUS

CHARLES P. RIES

I left it all: the paper and pens, publishers
and agents who could not love my inner
fantasy, and joined the circus.

The makeup, big nose, and fancy pants
helped me overcome my feelings of
obscurity. I created an identity grander
than my literary art. I now have something
worth writing about.

I married a fat lady; she gave birth to
a midget. I learned to swallow swords,
made friends with a contortionist who
told me to turn pens into pretzels,
and live, follow earth's bending curve.

IN THE DOORWAY

NORMAL

to Jack Micheline

you could hear him singing
7 a.m. / upper grant / 1971,
2 or 3. i'd be in the
doorway. he'd smell the
hangover / sense the
dying soul / the young
poet starving to crawl
out. he would stop just
long enough to sing me
"imma ol' cowhan', frem
de rio— —" — — "ah, buffalo
gals wontcha come ou'
tanight— —" etc. etc. — —
till i'd laugh. he'd wink
& be off down the street.
we never spoke.
they found jack at the
end of the line / where
that great heart of his
had probably been dreaming
a serenade into the dark
& quieting doorway.

POLITICUS

GUY R. BEINING

able to take pay dirt from pit of this century
& drag it with fishhooks into
the colosseum of glad baiters;
able to murder veins of fountains in the platz
& be the glare in cheney's glasses;
able to smell solar polaris in radius of bend,
shaking hands with bank vendors;
able to be in text of jazz
as fixture of white face basking in silver;
able to pour color into the mouth of surgeons tasting liver,
being that high hog of this century
already on its deathbed.

*

SIMON PERCHIK

Her death was reported for hours
on the weather channel
though it's not raining and you walk
slowly past the forecaster
who can't see you off some coast
the way a kitten just born
knows how to bathe itself
already curled over a saucer
filled with its mother and fur

—over the screen another storm
is forming, the clouds
come to an end, worn out
falling into the set as bedrock
never sure power will be restored
began again as water
that will not leave the sea—she died

while you were petting the waves
still on the glass canopy
warming it, walking in front
letting it wash over your lips
so nothing can be said
that is not rain—her death

was on a map where a face
should be though no one
except the darkness that always comes
asked or held her close.

REAL SOLUTION

GIOVANNI MALITO

So you become a rebel
loving with your mind,
revolting but destined to fail, fall
into seething conformity,
perhaps unwittingly
but it's all the same, structure.

Your solution, the solution,
without rigidity comes only
when you realize for yourself
just how far apart you must
place your imaginary walls, and
exactly when to let them fall.

HAYDEN CARRUTH SUITE

GLENN W. COOPER

1.

Carruth is dead,
the old man's long,
gray beard now
more than a
match for God's.

2.

Scrambled eggs &
whiskey in the
false dawn light,
the light inside
you now,
the whiskey &
the eggs scrambled
to pure infinity.

3.

In the nuthouse
looking out
at the tumult
of the wind
in the poplars,
but always seeing
more than just
wind & trees.
Seeing instead
the way we all
bend to circumstance.

4.

A lover of nature,
I imagine you a man
letting birds out
of cages,
rabbits from hutches.
Now, your turn.

5.

You wave from across
the wide river, wade
into death's pale nest,
something inside you
glad to be done with it
all, your hands small
and childlike again,
freed from their
mangled stroke-agony.

QUASI SETTANT'ANNI SONO TRASCORSI

FERRUCCIO BRUGNARO

a Federico Garcia Lorca

I giorni e le notti avevano
      il pallore
    di questi giorni e queste notti.
  C'era la luna clara di Cuba
        che smascherava
          il terrore dilagante.
I falangisti, i fascisti a Granada
        marciavano inferociti
          beffardi
            verso la tua casa.
     La giovane Repubblica di Spagna
          venne data alle fiamme.
Le tue grida intrise di sangue
        giunsero lontano
     si incrociarono, si strinsero
        alle mie grida
      in un'alba d'agosto
          senza eguali
        per bellezza e ferocia.
Il tempo non cancellò tutto
        il tempo.
    L'amore del tuo sogno
    la tua sete di libertà
    crebbero forte nelle nostre carni
      furono la nostra stessa vita.
Ma ora ... ora ... Federico carissimo
quasi settant'anni sono trascorsi ...
Il mondo è ancora infestato
        di insaziabili egoismi
      guerre
          fascism
     aumenta la follia

nel cervello umano.
Sulle strade d'Europa
che vacilla
si risentono di nuovo
gli schiamazzi
degli aguzzini
dei violenti
contro questo nostro cuore
risoluto determinato
a resistere
resistere
all'assassinio e alla morte.

SEVENTY YEARS HAVE PASSED

FERRUCCIO BRUGNARO

Translated from the Italian by JACK HIRSCHMAN

to Federico Garcia Lorca

The days and the nights have
                the pallor
        of those days and nights.
        There was Cuba's clear moon
                that unmasked
                        the spreading terror.
The falangists, the Grenada fascists
                those ferocious jokers
                        marched
                                toward your house.
        The young Republic of Spain
                        was put to the flames.
Your blood-soaked cries
                        would reach far away
                would cross and press
                        against my cry
                                in an August dawn
                                        unequaled
                        in beauty and ferocity.
Time can't erase all
                of time.
        The love of your dream
        your thirst for freedom
        grew strong in our flesh
                        were our very life.
But now ... now ... dearest Federico
almost seventy years have passed. ...
The world's still infested
                        with insatiable egoisms
                        wars

fascisms
madness increases
in the human brain.
On the streets of a Europe
that's wavering
the uproars
of the torturers
and violent ones
are on the rise again
against our heart
resolved and determined
to resist
resist
murder and death.

WIND–CHECKED

MIGNON ARIEL KING

This meal smells like someone else's,
faintly hinting of home and contentment,
vanilla steeped in old-oaked casks
for months, alcohol thawing sweet limbs.
Only one room in your dream creation.

Storm-split wood under our bare feet
is a wide-planked display of tongue
fitting groove, natural burls and plugs
from musket balls' penetration of bark.
Your fingers rubbed, caressed the grain.

All effort becomes disjointed now, where
the boards can be read as pages from a
history book. But our union, cabined all
winter, no fresher in spring, is simple:
only thing well-laid here is the floor.

FOR ALL THE YEARS

DAVID J. THOMPSON

The barmaid sits down once every week
to tell them a joke when she comes around
to collect their empties. Tonight, it's a long one
about a penguin, a seal, and a blowjob.
When she's done, they all laugh and
say, That's a good one, Linda, give her
high fives as she stands to gather an armful
of Pabst Blue Ribbon bottles from the table.

As soon as she's out of earshot, ones of them says,
I think she told that one a few months ago, another adds
that she could see the punchline coming a mile away,
and the real fat guy getting up for the men's room
reminds them that her jokes suck week after week
for all the years they've been coming to this dump.
They all nod, take a swallow from their beers in what seems
like unison, turn their attention to the pitcher winding up
on the big-screen TV at the other end of the bar as if they expect
some sort of play they've never seen before.

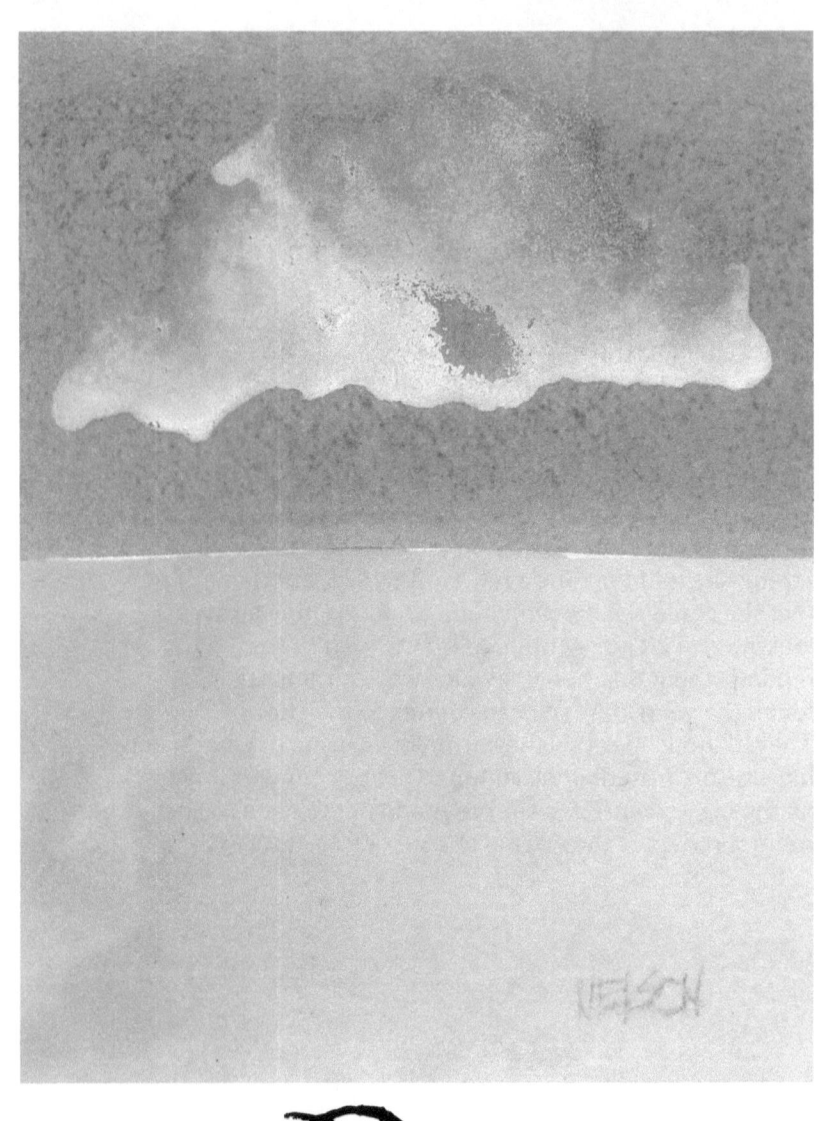

Poiesis

REVIEW
ISSUE THREE

ROSES

TIM SCANNELL

Sent a bushel basket of
Autumn leaves to her
(UPS: $10.50);
A box of wooden matches
(Safeway: $1.19), and
Enclosed the best love note
Ever penned:

"Ignore the city ordinance!"

AGE OF UNCERTAINTY

JOSEPH DORAZIO

We press on
beyond the pass
past the point of no return,
trespassers
paused upon
      a precipice—

CHILDREN OF MEMORY

BOB SHARKEY

Crisscross over slippery walkways.
Big white flakes fall, cling to the trees.
All is soft, muffled sounds, solemn.
A yellow light above the park inviting.
Up and in that light there's warmth,
big glass windows looking down.
A hothouse nurturing delicate memories.
Like that triggered by the boyish
Montagnard soldier on the wall. 1969.
Of another photographer, U.S. Army.
Assignment—document a dying way of life,
possibly the village of this very soldier.
The other photos here—even the colorful,
peaceful, contemporary, and post it all—
the young people in this room, right here
but unreal in some way, dream characters,
the daughters and sons of dreams
fertilize a full blooming of memory
settling finally on that photographer's body
floating facedown in a shallow lake.

THE MURDEROUS TENTACLES OF THE MOON

NORMAL

i reached for you last night
you turned the other way
you held another lover in your arms

it was the moon

i said
come back
i said i love you more than the moon

but you were gone
lost among the strangulation of moonbeams

& i heard the little murmurs of your act
& i heard the throes of its near completion
the groans of your special agony

i settled back

the long quiet
before the sun's reprieve

BETWEEN THE SILENCE

PATRICE M. WILSON

Between the music,
the beats in each measure,

between nothing
and the something arching through it,

a buttress, a bridge,
catching the something

before it winds itself
into a maze, a labyrinth

that must be erased
between what happens

and starting again—
before you reach

the top of the hill and look over,
the mark you make

in a book
to get to know it—

I will write to you,
ask for your friendship.

I am over a hill, looking outward.
I am as frail

as a puff of blue smoke.
I will keep you

between two eyelashes,
between two eyes,

in the midst of the stars,
between the silence.

TUTTI ASSOLTI PROCESSO PER LE MORTI AL PETROLCHIMICO

FERRUCCIO BRUGNARO

Lavoravamo tra micidiali veleni
                    sostanze terribili
                            cancerogene.
Non affermate ora
                furfanti
                        ladri di vite
        che non c'era alcuna certezza
            che non c'erano legislazioni.
Non dite, non dite che non sapevate.
Avete ammazzato e ammazzate ancora
                        tranquilli indisturbati
            tanto
                    il fatto non sussiste.
I miei compagni morti non sono
                            mai esistiti
                    sono svaniti nel nulla.
        I miei compagni operai
                        morti
                    non possono tollerare
                        questa vergogna.
Non possiamo sopportare
                        questo insulto.
        Nessun padrone
                nessun tribunale
    potrà mai recingerci
                    di un così grande
        infame silenzio.

ALL ACQUITTED IN TRIAL OVER PETROCHEMICAL DEAD

FERRUCCIO BRUGNARO

Translated from the Italian by JACK HIRSCHMAN

We worked in the midst of deadly poisons
                    awful cancerous
                              substances.
Don't you bastards you
              robbers of life
                        now insist
       that there was no assurance
       that there were no laws.
Don't say, don't say you didn't know.
You've murdered and still murder
                        calmly coolly
         because
              what you did doesn't exist.
My dead comrades
              never existed
       they've disappeared in nothingness.
My comrades dead
              workers
              can't stand
                    this shame.
We can't tolerate
              this insult.
       No boss
              no court
   ever could fence us in
                    with such a huge
       rotten silence.

SIMON PERCHIK

And for the first time, begins
till even today all water
longs to escape with the sun

the way the dead have been taught
and once on shore
wait for the waves to open again

as flowers smelling from salt
and lips and readiness
—it's not by accident

blood at the slightest chance
will run away
though not every wound

can be traced back to the sharp turn
and circling down into stones
by the mouthfuls—you taste a sea

stained by faraway nights
and teeth then loneliness
and not one star is spared

—by morning the throbbing
is at home in your heart
brings it closer and closer

as if a sister sun, not yet visible
rises inside the months, years, oceans
and what you carry off

is the silence they once were
silent and covered with smoke
no longer struggling or grass.

GOD LOVES ROCK

JOHN BERBRICH

God loves rock music
He hates big corporate arena rock
Like REO and Styx

But He loves Rock, especially
Punk rock

He loves the underfed, angular
Guitar players
The screaming singers
The razor-sharp guitar riffs
Blasting into the quiet air
Of His green Earth

God loves the songs about A.D.D.
And the whole world
On heroin, the organization
Of punks into a shouting army

He doesn't quite understand all the words
But He turns up the volume
Just a notch
And hums along with
A shrieking freak
Who wants to exchange his guts
For something a little more eternal

CONTAGIOUS

STEPHANIE HITESHEW

They all call me ugly.
I tell them,
"If that's true,
I hope it's contagious."
And they scatter
like the days
I wasn't this smart.

THE SHELLEY SENRYU

HARLAND RISTAU

then what is life, cried the poet?
just waiting for the next calamity
to come around, cried Mary!

LETTER TO THE EDITOR OF OUR SMALL-TOWN NEWSPAPER

PATRICK MCKINNON

" ... at the monthly Poetry Harbor readings
where would-be poets gather to read their writing
to anyone willing to listen ... "
—Duluth News-Tribune, *March 1991*

dear editor
last week i was called
a would-be poet
in yr news
paper
by one of yr aspiring
journalismists

so editor
it's well known
especially by you & me
would-be poets
work at news
papers

& pomz come
squirting out of me
like singing dancing turds
i leave steaming
on discarded copies
of yr news
paper

sincerely
patrick mckinnon
actual poet

LOST IN THOUGHT

GIOVANNI MALITO

What would our world be like
had Hitler gone to art school?
had the Mensheviks been pink?
had Chiang Kai-shek not been such an asshole?
had the Americans not drunk tea?
had Saul not become St. Paul
but upon falling from his donkey
been run down by the oncoming traffic
and squashed beyond redemption?

GANGSTA' STYLE

ZOE A. JAIMOT

for Tupac

Back in the day of crack fiends, black queens,
    and prettyass Mercedes ride machines ...

He was a playah a brother a fuckin mother

He was a young soulpartymastah makin, fightin
    all in heavy calibers of music rappin ...

He lived and died by a 9mm cap like his fine rap

Sure you tried to jail him, dis him,
    but you never could dismiss him ...

With secret hand signals he spoke his rhyme

Never jonesin but fightin back, with a knack,
    with words always like gunfire on the attack ...

Talkin trash nonstop to the cops put his records on top

Which moved even pure Caucasians, on occasion,
    to get down in hiphop animation ...

Wearin that littleass goatee and crass scowl

Your view of life, one of constant strife,
    expressions and images carved with a cutting knife ...

Bodybags full of revolutionary spirit, can you hear it

Wu Tang and Dr. Dre, by degree, poor facsimiles
    of the riots you created all on CD ...

So when you axsked him to ride y'shouldah jes stepped aside

On those streets you cruised dead set, composing epithets,
       wonderin who would take the final bullet ...

You had your people, dogs, crew strutting down that avenue

In a code created by you, shots ring out, all about,
       drive-by shootings of words throughout ...

In darker prisons of shadow where homies waited for DR to show

How they could abuse you, how they would finally shoot you,
       but we ain't ever gonna lose you ...

And yeah, they threw down on you, killed you, chilled you

We know you played hard, you played fast,
       tattooed to a body that wouldn't last ...

Getting tingly with his words you still adore him abhor him

And it's elementary as the penitentiary,
       nothin to it but to do it
       cuz this verse and episode's never ended.

SOUNDS OF SUNLIGHT

NEAL WILGUS

A beeping something
is backing up in the alley
with the dull roar
of the traffic
as accompaniment.
Kids are yelling
and throwing rocks
with police sirens
in the background
rounding things out.
Wind in the trees
and screams in the distance.
Gunfire or backfire
or both
punctuate the composition—
then running footsteps,
angry voices, accusations.
A plane goes over
and when it passes
a 'copter thuds down
and the beeper
backs up again.

THE END

MICHAEL KRIESEL

The man
who is writing
the end of the world
began like this

he sat down
in a chair
beside a window
closed his eyes
& waited for the steam
to finish rising from
a cup of coffee

pen & paper resting
on the windowsill

darkness spreading
from behind some trees
outside the window

the trees are an aquamarine

what kind of trees they are is unimportant

what's important
is the way already it's begun

how every night
behind his eyes
a few less stars come out

JUST ANOTHER WORD

PAMELA ANNAS

for Janis Joplin, 1943-1970

1969. I'm tossing back bourbon
and dancing alone in my living room
to your smoky chain-link barbed-wire voice
biting off chunks of pain.

White girl from Texas growling out the blues,
channeling Big Mama Thornton and Bessie,
the way they rode the blues migration north
to Chicago and New York off the front porches
out of honky tonks and Vaudeville tents
into Saturday night bright lights
and everyone's house
through
      the miracle
           of the windup
               Victrola.
They rewrote what women could do—
and the price.

Forty years later, thumbing your nose
at Port Arthur, Texas, you sped out of town
on a Sixties road trip to North Beach and the Haight,
mixed blues, rock, and the beats to sing your throat raw:
     We may not be here tomorrow, no
        I'd say get it while you can

Voice big as the Texas sky, explosive as an oil well on fire
voice of shivers, sugar, and Southern Comfort
brown velvet and white horse, needles and nettles
pounding summer sun and never
quite fitting in.

Take another little piece of my heart now, baby.
Break it.

THE MANY BRIDGES

DAVID J. THOMPSON

My slow summer of chemotherapy ends
Labor Day weekend high up in a Pittsburgh hotel.
My girlfriend in her black dress has
Bill Evans playing "My Foolish Heart"
on my laptop, pours room-service champagne
as we watch the slow, certain sunset
behind the hills and on the Allegheny River
outside the window. She leans over and
kisses me softly on top of my bald head
as the lights come on across the many bridges.
"It's beautiful tonight, isn't it?" she says,
and I move to hold her, feel her close to me,
the opening gesture of now an unsure autumn.

FEATURED
WRITER

T. KILGORE SPLAKE

LONG WHITE MUSINGS

winter evening darkness
frosty breath steaming
old man on nightly hike
graybeard poet
deep in december tides
bootsteps crunching
arctic long hike
misty dreams
pretty girl lover
never found
april motorcycle fevers
vincent "black lightning"
brit cc's jazzing cojones
fading distant light
grizzled bardic survivor
youth wives hospital stays
hated millstone career
alcoholic suicide dance
avoiding seductive nothingness
garden golf
television vegetable
soon back home
art gallery attic sanctuary
alone in nighttime quiet
sipping warm bitter ale
soft incense aromas
muse light whispers
words becoming music
early tomorrow waking
wild tiger
roaring in his skull

BEING

black fog rising

moving off superior

auto-tranny petrol fill

bottle of jack between legs

white line fevers

jeffers
snyder
under the milkwood
rimbaud
baudelaire
trout fishing in america
robert service

bob wills
"two hanks"
patsy patsy patsy cline

grand canyon rendezvous

elvis
kerouac
"tricky dick" nixon

existential "mama's boys"

lost brothers
cold distant fathers
dark angry moods
desire to make others notice

later finding

modoc warrior "captain jack"

ghost guide to winter retreat

puerto sanato   cassady's ghost
cuernavaca   under the volcano
iguana nights   burton liz

galapagos

watching turtles hatch

madly racing gulls

ocean tides sanctuary

BECOMING

graybeard bardic soul

standing eight count

on road to oz

cold dark alone

musing

that was then this is now

WHAT TO DO

plastic insurance card binge
odd 40s b+w films
alky brain cell suicide
grand sexual orgy
ask nun's blessings
jack armstrong's "wheaties"

mad man giving away possessions

finding wooing woodland witch

liking idea

time doesn't exist

denying nursing home confusion

diaper
wheelchair
toothless
blind
lysol stink

good day rallies

waiting sign telling inspiration

"it is now"

dancing naked

loose long hair flowing

beyond

existing metes and bounds

return to womb

end of the earth

coyote
catfish
raven
bluebottle fly

companions

knowing grinning smile

smooth pale bone

spring

roadkill skull

COME IN RANGOON

holter monitor lines
revealing dangerous arrhythmia
serious problem
with big heart muscle
graybeard poet telling
local doctor
"i will not
make an ambulance trip"
riding to marquette hospital
cardiovascular specialists
young tommy
growing up with
generation of "flying tigers"
not afraid of dying
like "pappy" boyington
"black mac" mcgarry
aces chasing jap zeroes
protecting burma road
wearing leather jackets
chinese flag
with "blood chit"
message for help
if shot down
flying claire chennault's
p-40's with tiger teeth
kunming yunfu luichow
artful dodger
turning steady miles
engine smooth hummmm
warm cockpit
relaxed hand on throttle
earplugs goggles oxygen mask
wondering about god
survival of one's soul
thinking of love
young girls lost
married women divorced
sons and daughter
mother and father memories

determined survivor
toughing out whatever
getting surgery
returning to my
god's country home
rehabbing quickly
still time to write
new novel manuscript
quiet season of "long white"
early winter mornings
contesting ever elusive
damn dame lady muse
one more time

WHEN I GO

JOE SPEER

I don't want to be planted
in a buff graveyard
or
have friends
disperse my cremains
over Bixby Bridge
I want to disappear in toto
into a novel or film
I'll join
John Dos Passos'
Three Soldiers
and feel proud
with Andrews
to desert from
the faceless automation
army
I'll investigate
Remembrance of Things Past
for Marcel Proust
and ferret out the
clandestine affairs
of Albertine
I'll grin with Lewis Carroll
as *Alice in Wonderland*
accepts
the curiosity
of imagination
I'll have a chat
with the loving
and honest Alyosha
in Dostoevsky's
final novel
The Brothers Karamazov
with *Junior Bonner*
I'll ride the wild bull
until the buzzer rings
in *Hunchback of Notre Dame*

I'll dance
with gypsy girl Esméralda
in *One P.M., Sweet Toronto*
I'll play
rhythm guitar
with John Lennon
and the Plastic Ono Band
in *The Getaway*
I'll wear body armor
and rob a bank
then buy a truck
and escape
into Mexico
in *Downhill Racer*
I'll speed for Olympic gold
with Robert Redford
when my checkout time arrives
I want my lapse into
a mode of quiescence
the subtle smile of Buddha
free of attachment
and when friends ask
my whereabouts
my executors will say
"he was last seen in
The Dharma Bums
hiking a mountain trail
to visit Kerouac
in a remote fire tower"

SILVER BIRCH

MARY GUCKIAN

Silver birch trees burst billowing
dirndl skirts while gusts of wind
shake layers of green flounces
on top of tall stilts: exposing
my desk to crosswinds, blustering
air shudders my body to life.

Struggling with the computer I ease
my thoughts into ordering books on
recycled paper for the library stock.

During the day silver skin glows
on firm trunks: sun brightens space,
under heavy green cloaks, on branches
widening out year after year, adorning
empty space outside Victorian windows.

RIGHT FOOT INTO WINGS

CHARLES P. RIES

My worst curse—immobility.
Crutches and no car for six weeks.
The basement writing room has
become a sensory-deprivation chamber.

Even my pain medication haunts me—
midgets in white doctors' jackets chasing
me with whips offering me more pills.

All I can do is—hop, hop, hop.

"You needed this," Elaine tells me.
"A divine light will appear, a voice in
the night, an angel will come, you'll be
forever changed. You want to change,
don't you? You could use a little changing,
you know. Think transubstantiation's easy?
Huh? Do you? How about making the move
from caterpillar to butterfly? Think that's
so easy? Stop complaining and be glad
you have one good foot."

No pity down here in the deprivation chamber.
        Shut up and take it like a man.
                Life's a trash can—deal with it.

Alone in the basement—hop, hop, hop.
Entertaining pain medication dwarfs—hop, hop, hop.
Writing fiction only a fleeting idea—hop, hop, hop.

Six weeks until transubstantiation liftoff.
        Fly to Mexico amidst clouds of Monarchs.
                Butterfly wings better than any right foot.

YARDWORK

GARY EVERY

My longest account
has been with Mrs. Wigston.
When her yard is overrun
with grasses, weeds, and wildflowers
she asks me to landscape
her parcel of earth.
Armed only with a hoe
I wield the wrath of my blade
until the soil is barren.
Her payment is always prompt
but paperclipped with a note complaining
that I have left behind too many wildflowers.

"After the bloom has died,
a wildflower is just another ugly weed."

Every year there are a few more wildflowers.
Mrs. Wigston is my oldest client
but it is a slow revolution
when one must wait
for a harvest of seeds.

BACKING UP A TRAILER

GUY R. BEINING

subtitled: that sweet home
where nobody roams.
the cure is lost & unknown again
watching down & out poets drink
in & out of sketchy scenes
as a leading academic poet
runs thru mirrored halls seeing
only the flying pieces of himself,
but nobody will bring
him back together again.
it is the last ride,
the last bout,
the last touching of people
that sit in academic suits
& photocopy their sculptured hands.
there is etiquette here without belief,
emily post in post-op,
so back up the trailer
into the sweet home of no one
& make your literary pitch.

UNITED SHINERS OF ARTIFICE

JUSTIN ROGERS

who are these people
this strange tribe of gatherers of
     all things that shine

who wander in a darkness
lit only by the garish glare
of now's neon lines

what manner of people are these
who pray to and prey on
loot hunt and gather
     all things that shine

where are the children
of the tribe of
     all things that shine

have they been rounded up
sold off and sold out
mortgaged away
dealt for derivatives
traded
     for things that shine

brokered into bondage
sent to global sweatshops
credit default swapped
indentured
     for things that shine

where are the children
of the tribe of
     all things that shine

who do they sing lullabies to

GARAGE SALE

LILA GOODMAN

A shiny black stool
2 tarnished brass wastebaskets
pocketbooks, pages yellowed.
I bought *The Red Pony*
by John Steinbeck.
Light blue dishes
white dishes with a rose pattern
old-fashioned pots
a frying pan with a black handle
a floor lamp with an off-white
taffeta shade, a worn green plaid
loveseat, a red director's chair
a navy-blue velvet pillow
have they been hidden from sight of mind
drinking glasses of various sizes
an unused photo album
a terrible oil painting
of a blue vase with yellow roses
a cookie jar in the shape of a cat
a rack of blue jeans, blouses,
sweaters, men's jackets and trousers,
men's old-fashioned brown-leather shoes,
rubber thongs, a pair of pink fluffy
ladies' slippers, tan bath towels
from the Biltmore Hotel
a white cook's apron, cheap jewelry
a ruby ring, fake gold bracelets
a string of pearls, and an old black
manual Royal typewriter that I
tried just for fun.

All on the lawn, going for nothing,
half an apartment, half a life.

Poiesis

REVIEW

ISSUE FOUR

SAKS FIFTH AVENUE

CHARLES P. RIES

Time moves so slowly as we wait for
our loved ones to exit the dressing room
—again.

Exotic birds parade before us
Tight fitting
      Low riding
            Up lifting
                  Miracle bras
Moving in synchronous motion
            from rack to stack.

My male comrades and I
            warm the bench.
We're the second stringers.
Shoes
      Accessories
            Lingerie
                Lipstick
                    Eyeshadow.
You exit a new woman.

CHAMPAGNE DAWN

ARTHUR WINFIELD KNIGHT

I open a bottle of champagne
shortly before dawn.
Kit and I drink it
from lead crystal glasses
as we watch the dark fade
to amethyst. I remember
drinking martinis at dawn
when I was dating Veronica
50 years ago in San Francisco,
the sky a bloody rose,
the air like ozone. In those days
we drank from jelly glasses.
Everything is different,
but not much changes.

RAW
WAR

GUY R. BEINING

stepping stones ... stopping,
suddenly afraid, finding that
the rewind button is stuck.

one cannot find a place today
that is not shot apart,
& between all the hills
of piled up & twisted forms
is a landscape that squints
not from fabled terrorism
but the constant presence of a
consumer-filled consumptive war.

HEROES, VILLAINS, & OTHER ENTERTAINERS

NORMAL

"Everything is miraculous.
It is a miracle that one does not melt in one's bath."
—Pablo Picasso

once knew this jack been a guard to the
shit who shot john lennon.
told me the prisoners loved to sing up
the old beatles songs whenever chapman
came within earshot;
a prisoner's custom passed on
generation to generation—
they all became a george, a ringo,
a john, & a paul
—some sentences fit the crime.

once saw jerry lee lewis in concert.
the late-in-life idol sang with the
aggregate joy of a withering pod;
hissed his backup,
snarled his audience. the ushers
had to keep him from running off.
i chanced by the stage door as
a single cop led *the killer* out;
no crowd
no autographs
no applause; just a colossal black
limousine into which this shrunken old
man faded into a language of wax & smoke.
another statue of a childhood icon
disappearing on the mantelpiece of memory.

face your demons head on.
avoid your heroes like the plague.

once traveled with a caravan of 5 vulgar
vaudevillians known to no one as the
"leon football marching band."
they were sots.
i was a sot.
we were monstrously successful at the
mystical point of returning insignificance.
their rallying mantra had it
i would never live long enough to see in
1973.
that was 1972.

35 years later i remain the final member
of the "leon football marching band."

an aging anachronism
the last vulgarian
who has forgotten the punchline

to a bad joke.

THE URBAN CLAUSTROPHILE

ARNOLD SKEMER

In little spaces do we delve
Making much of a few square feet.
Expensive land values force us into corners
As we make use of strange angles
Hewn out of remnants of the hellish grid.

Constriction leads us to our devices
And compression lends a resourcefulness with space.
Spatial oddity enforces eccentricity with area
And forces us into corners of infinite possibility.

Placed in close proximity with each other
We inure ourselves with propinquity
And find terror in broad expanses
Abhorring Kansan prairies for small boxes
Of fetid air, stinking of our own exhalations,
Our own farts, our own body aroma.

We come to adore these little spaces,
Embellishing them, augmenting them
With the creations of our singular inventiveness
And instead of fear we live in their embrace
Dwelling in restricted space.

*

Not the paper you write on
yet your arms are warmed
the way each mother all night

will feed her child's first cry
open one breast for food
the other without a sound

though you can still make out
where the flames are coming from
once these flowers are unwrapped

and singing all at once
as cradlesong—you almost hear
the hot coals freezing in midair

closer and closer to one another
—you never forget this hunger
and in your mouth ice.

GOOD NIGHT

LILA GOODMAN

I need a seatbelt
when I sleep.
Rolling and turning,
falling out of bed,
sleepwalking, nightmares,
waking up screaming,
my nightgown damp with sweat.
Noting the clock
with the luminous dial,
turning, turning to sleep.

The dreams are frustrating
and frightening: a serpent's
head, my car lost, a prowler
in the house, the handsome man
in the blue suit, my mother,
again and again my mother.

I sleep alone now
in my twin bed, the heavy
quilt, the bed pad that's
a little lumpy, the cool sheet,
the window open slightly.

I enter the bed each night
with trepidation. It's sort of
like a movie thriller for me.
I'm there at the appointed time.
The room is dark. I'm a little scared;
I never know what's going to happen.

MAJESTIC ICON

I love to stand in the graveyard,
underneath the hanging branches
of the old palm tree—
its: broad arms sheltering
headstones that inform—
of lives that are now at peace.

At funerals, I hide from showers
under the sprawling limbs
of this majestic icon—
where earth is dry, protected
from hailstones and hot sun: below
this sacred tree tranquility reigns.

QUALITY TIME

TIM SCANNELL

I use time with obsessive
Care only once during the day:
Getting butter to every corner,
Every goddamned edge of
The toast.

A PLACE

BRUCE MCRAE

The sun is a red triangle.
The town is frayed silk,
tucked away in the burlap forests.

Clouds go for jaunty hayrides,
sneak in a little smooching,
sing the company song in Mandarin.

Ghosts for policemen,
and they ride the skeletons of horses
(thus the glassy horseshoes).

The misty-eyed cottages ...
Someone's drawn monkey faces
on their papery windows.

They've left a fuzzy paw
in the voice-laden mailbox.
Their bad breaths are knocking.

Under the tipsy streetlamp
a blind cockroach, a one-man band,
a dancing harmonica.

In the barber's chair, a raindrop.
In the pub, dust playing chess.
In the library, novels mulling it over.

At night a black moon rolls in.
We huddle 'round a matchstick,
the world coming down on us hard

The world coming.

FEATURED
WRITER

ROBERT SCHULER

FOR GEOFFREY HILL, BECKETT, AND BLAKE

this is not Canaan   this is chaos
far beyond reason
in communion we drink
mezcal   falling under spells
drowning ourselves
in the wide mirrors of stares
the drums of revolution muted
to a slow circling dance
led by El Caudillo
the tigers of wrath die
strangled in asylums
the horses of dissent rush
wilder into the red desert

AFTER ANTONIONI

we do not see
the rose beauty of the bricks
framed in the late-winter windows
at the end of the long halls
vines dangling down
green in cold blue air
in the living room where we dance
rugs patterned silver
with scimitars   scarlet with fires
ethereally purple-blue violets
no stars tonight   moon down
a night of ice
a night of love

APRÈS MOI, LE DÉLUGE, IN CELEBRATION OF ANOTHER NEW YEAR, 2009

I've been thinking
about rapping out a sermon
a hip ad   a placard   a medallion
a bumper sticker a pennant a certificate
a garish banner a Hallmark card
for all of us who have made
fascism
            possible in our times

MILESTONES

Bach-like again and again
and again   the Pharoanic
grace and power of Coltrane's saxophone
blasting sands and dust away
shuddering us alive

WAR CHANT

I speak for the liberation of the soul
from the slavery of the marketplace

SKIING, MARCH 8TH

I'm alone in the clear light of the late afternoon
skis rattling across scarred patches of ice
cedar waxwings scrambling in the leaves
the naked thickets   seeking berries
above the just-unlocked river
ice-breakers will bust up the frozen
father of waters this Tuesday
mallards honking boating downriver
icicles fall from the cliffs
scattering black dust into the winds

PARIS / BERKELEY

streets of dreams
everything open   the wide night
bookshops   bins of thumbed
thin old books   New Directions
Gallimard   Black Sparrow
sipping brandy
you could read Rimbaud and Reverdy
under the streetlamps
Montmartre   Solesmes
hills sloping streets
walking   moons above
and below bobbing in the water
Art Blakey's Jazz Messengers
playing "Close Your Eyes"
anarchic in love

UNDERSTANDING ANITA

BOB SHARKEY

If a hurricane, Ophelia.
Sensing someone behind
watching her hips swivel
beneath the long dress.
A half-turn of the head,
dark, plain, firm profile,
the steady look that says,
"You'll do what I want."

If a city, New Orleans.
Not a cold, virtuous doer
of occasional good deeds.
Loved for being free
of guile and greed.
Innocent despite the fog
of alcohol and smoke.
A salty tear of the sea.

If anything, the tide.
Water catching dull green
from a cannery wall,
tossing it into a brightness.
She stands in unraked sand
looking out at the foam
tinged with red, blood
of the coming storm.

STICKING AROUND

DENIS SHEEHAN

A patchwork of staples and thumbtacks
Landscapes the circumference of a telephone pole
Once entrusted to affix various notices
And announcements
Lost Pets, Yard Sales
Local Fundraisers
Cockeyed thumbtacks mimic dead suns
Setting over the tiny, deformed bridges of metal
With the signs long removed by people
Or fallen to the weather
The staples and thumbtacks remain
Bringing to their host a blight
Protruding like skin tags
From an old man's underarm
Placed like crowns
Atop their respective wood-staining streaks of rust

STATUTORILY SPEAKING

BILL COSTLEY

A weary, stony Abe Lincoln
slumps as he reads a newspaper,
slowly speaking over his shoulder
toward the Statue of Liberty.

Abe: "Libby, will you please
wash those boys' mouths out
with some good American soap?"

Fatboys in shorts crowd around her,
spewing truly deranged slogans:

Fatboys: "Don't listen to Father Abe!"
"Obama's a Communist! Obama's Hitler!"
"Gov'mint wants to kill the soldiers";
"Gov'mint wants to kill the old";
"Abortion leads to euthanasia."

Liberty quickly fills up an enormous tin-tub
with boiling water & foaming pink liquid soap.
Raving Fatboys scatter fast.

WHAT MAKES JANE DOE TICK?

MIGNON ARIEL KING

She is definitely not alive, yet her presence fills the room,
stuffs it even fuller than the pamphlets, medical books,
and beanbag monkeys, bunnies, that fill the high shelves.
Even more distracting than him—the too-good-looking
doctor that women's magazines warn against. I do pay

attention to the "Everything is fine" follow-ups, pretend
I'll become a normal woman again someday, despite
the limitation of scars. But over every word and noise
in the comforting space of a mind that knows its business
is the sound of ticking that's behind her anatomy chart.

OLDER WOMEN

JOE SPEER

my girlfriend Fran and I
made an agreement—
I'd support us
to enable her immersion
in academia to earn
a degree in journalism
as a latecomer to education.
I became her mother's chauffeur
as Memaw desisted from driving
after knocking over three mailboxes.
upon returning home
at midnight from my job
my girlfriend asleep
Memaw listened for the
sibilant screen door.
I'd pull a chair next to her bed
while she recounted highlights
of a basketball game.
Fran's college days were hectic—
late-night sessions on newspaper
to meet deadlines
up early to attend class
flying to major cities
for conferences.
I saw more of her mother—
she was always available.
if love depends on time
shared together
then I loved Memaw more.
my girlfriend graduated
and began a stint
with the daily newspaper.
she made time to garden
and create tasty meals.
when Memaw died
we emptied out the house
and turned it over to

a realty company.
Fran suggested
we could live on her
social security and rental
if we could keep expenditures
to minimalist levels.
the prospect of living as a kept man—
a live-in retainer
stimulated my wanderlust.
we began with a trip to New Orleans.
I wanted to start
a Sunday at Café du Monde
then attend a cathedral service
then hit the Maple Leaf Bar
for the 3 p.m. open mic
and end the night
in a sex club on Bourbon Street.
there are advantages
to older women.

MAYONNAISE FARM

JUSTIN ROGERS

Having a photographic memory
      does not prevent one from forgetting

To expose the image
      to the light of truth

Thus, perhaps, twisting our sense
of actuality and morality
into a psychedelic mirage
as hazy as half-white lietruths

That fail to convey
the supreme meaning
of real fantasies, and
      fantastic realities

Thereby, limiting our fancifully dishonest
corporate propaganda-fed hallucinatory
quasi-knowledge-based perceptions to

Nothing more than dust
      blowin in the wind

Finally, rendering us deaf and mute
      in the face of life's ultimate question

Is this a warm rain, or
      am I being pissed on?

SOMETIMES CELEBRITIES

ZACK KOPP

sneak through our cities in 30-foot limos
with tinted windows   eluding the riot of jealous eyes
     they fancy in their guilt   and so make real
sniffing coke from silver platters and groping their plastic girls
behind the dark glass
   as outside men with the faces of lions
grasp bottles in paper sacks and laugh up blood in alleyways

and women like wolves beckon lewdly with fingers like hooks
   spitting out worms and rats

   the celebrities crane their necks
to catch all the weird scenes on the street
        but they can't get out
  the natives would tear them to shreds

   and the way inside is very tight
     so it works out nearly even

STOP ALLA GUERRA

FERRUCCIO BRUGNARO

Non aspettate che sia
        troppo tardi.
Non tacete, non tacete più.
    I missili
    le bombe
    stanno prendendo
        il sopravvento
sull'interno universo
        sull'intera vita.
Mostruosi animali hanno preso
        le redini
    della terra
        e del mondo.
L'oscuramento della mente
    e dell'anima
    è quasi
        totale.
Non tacete, non tacete oltre.
    La guerra solo parla
        forte alta
    in queste ore
  cospargendo città e pianure
  di fiammate di sangue
        e di morte.
Non tacete, non tacete ancora.
Il cuore umano aggredito
    dal terrore
        delle tenebre
in questi giorni
come un bimbo inerme
    annaspa
in un pianto estremo.

STOP THE WAR

FERRUCCIO BRUGNARO

Translated from the Italian by JACK HIRSCHMAN

Don't wait till it's
                too late.
Don't stay silent, not anymore.
            The missiles
            the bombs
            are getting
                    the upper hand
on the whole universe
                on all of life.
Monster animals have taken
                            the reins
                of earth
                        and world.
The darkening of the mind
                and soul
                is almost
                        total.
Don't clam up, don't stay silent.
            Only war talks
                        strong and loud
                in these hours
            spreading blazes of blood
            and death
                    in city and plain.
Don't be silent, don't keep still.
The human heart assaulted
                    by the terror
                            of darkness
these days
like a defenseless child
                    flounders
in uttermost weeping.

AMPHITHEATER

GARY EVERY

I am stalking wild turkeys
trying to capture the perfect photograph,
a big tom with bronze feathers and bright red comb
but the silly pudgy bird proves elusive.
I turn deeper into the forest
traveling further and further
between the trees,
giant trees towering high above my head.
Gobbling calls haunt me as I walk,
turkeys roosting in the treetops,
hidden in the shadows,
until I stumble upon
an old abandoned cabin
and just beyond that

a long-forgotten amphitheater.
Here, the trees have been sacrificed,
sawed and planed to make boards
then nailed into benches
arranged in rows like church pews.
The little stage is made of stone
old geological bones
covered with moss and lichen,
a few rocks tumbled out of place.

How strange to stumble upon this location
while I am lost in the woods.
I consider myself a storyteller,
and stand on the stage,
words falling from my tongue
like newborn rain.
Gradually ghosts fill the pews,
a thousand faceless warriors
whispering dialogue of yesteryore
echoes of my hero's tale,
while ahead and behind me the river
continuously flows.

RODENTIA

GEORGE HELD

Learn to live with rodents
They're with us everywhere—

The mouse in the pantry
The squirrel in the yard

The rat in the alley
The boss in the office

ALL THE YEARS WASTED

ROSS VASSILEV

like cum in a toilet
like endless cloudy afternoons
while the kid
upstairs
jumps up and down
all the years wasted
like headless mice in the yard
like broken blond
Barbie dolls in landfills
like America buried under
mountains of garbage
like the endless mindless noise
on the TV
(I don't even mean the commercials)
like the Christians burning
Sappho
like the birth of America
or death in Hollywood
Marilyn Monroe lying facedown
in her bed
her big white ass
in the air.

THE ASSAULT OF NUN PLASTICITY

KEZ PANEL

the aroma of warm buttered biscuits and olive-oiled chicken breasts
fills my personal space like an invisible layer of evening aftershave,
while his short nimble fingers from the business end of his jabbing
   elbows
start striking and grabbing at my plastic lady in black
and playing with her all-too-familiar thimbled buttocks. ...
she is the jack kerouac of the choir, made of fine italian porcelain,
and carried in small burlap sacks and cotton pockets and leather
   satchels.
never once complaining of the religious innuendos from the drunk
   cook,
only to digest his insulting mockery ... and to puke up a rainbow!

IMAGES IN THE DARK

PATRICE M. WILSON

I. Death Plague

The universe snapped shut
the night a skeleton walked
among soft women
who should have been singing
lullabies to a maiden asleep
on a marble divan,

the skeleton's thin wife dressed
with the air of lonely penthouse
dwellers who would wear red and
wait for excitement like tonight—

but the skeleton wanted the virgin
this time, canceling the cosmos
for spite,
soft women lifting their arms up
to the sky for help.

II. Life from Death

A dragon-drawn chariot rescues Medea;
later, Wotan's daughters ride
through clouds' smoldering fury,
huge furrowed eyebrows over
bare rough-edged mountains,
valleys abandoned by light
in the view of a bloodshot eye
blinking with lightning,
windy with thunderbolts
while a pregnant woman sleeps
in a cave.

III. Innocence and Evil

After the attack by demons,
a thousand saints processed,
their line of candles
bobbing up and down in twilight,
their thin lives glowing almost fleshless
as churches filled with their tragedy.

Not out of this will come the day
when small children play
with deadly serpents; the parents,
wise, not moving, watch the snakes
eventually go their own way.

IV. The Beginning, Again

Certain pine trees in the snow were illumined;
no one knew where the light came from,
a puzzle of black rocks cracked open
summoning primal shining dreams,
edges that had once touched
and come, fast, together.

YOUNG SAILORS

MICHAEL KRIESEL

Drinking Mad Dog
cut with 7-Up
behind the laundromat

wishing it was
Friday night

WAITING FOR THE LINE

HENRY DENANDER

I am leaning against the wall, reading the magazine I picked up on the train. I'm watching the house on the other side of the street. It's big and the door impressive; the large stone inscription over the door reads *Tag Members Only*, and the stone looks very old, older than the house itself. All the windows are barred, and there is nothing happening outside, no one entering or coming out. I am waiting for the coffee shop to open, and I will sit at the window table with my notebook, where I have a good view of the house and its doorway. I've been trying to write for months; I used to be able to jot down ideas for poems all through the day, and there was always something grabbing my attention.

Here I am, across the street from the mansion-like building, ordering coffee, staring out the window and checking the entrance. I know that if I sit here long enough, everything will come back to me, and slowly, I will see a line forming, outside The House of Tags.

ISSUE FIVE

SUGGESTION BOX

RAY LARSEN

Every day upon entering the coliseum,
     I see it
Well-crafted from exotic hardwoods
Stolen, I'm sure, from some forest primeval
Hand-polished brass hardware makes certain
All submissions remain confidential
Goddamn thing probably cost more than
      I make in a week

Passing by, I project poison through the dark slot
A gill of gall in your hogshead of cream
The unspoken knowledge that if I told you what
     I really thought
The linoleum floor would rend beneath your feet
You would become helplessly entangled
In basement chains and sour mop heads—things
      you know nothing about

My first suggestion would be to get rid of that box

LASSO

APRIL MICHELLE BRATTEN

On Saturday nights
he would gather my long hair,
whipping it like a lasso.

Annihilated,
I was blasted into a thousand pieces,
blackened limp beneath his thrusting feet.

I was not dead,
but a dying, soulless pile of soot
waiting to be blown away.

I learned to harden, and build new bones,
leak blue flames.

My new throat is a dry desert.
I do not cry.

I watch the cinders that fall,
not mine, but his,
the remnants of a stone man's lost eloquence.

Oh, damp spot,
you were once home to my blood,
but now you are drying as a fig.

I roll you under bare feet,
slap at you with dry palms,

and release my body from you who blames it.

THE WINTER HOME
OF MONARCHS

DONOVAN WHITE

They'd sought for more than twenty years
The winter home of butterflies.
The migratory mystery, longstanding, elusive—
All sealed in native xenophobic superstition.

A hurricane of millions,
Ascendant souls, per acre.

He's colorblind, can't see the seething symphony
Of orange and black on mountain cedar,
To cloak the conifers in tremblant wings
And soar a cloud of tigers in the mariposa light.

WHERE GREASY DUCKTAILS ARE SMOOTHED INTO PLACE

ZACK KOPP

at stoplights and "drunk Indians"
lie in the road with their feet cut off.
The street stinks with an eerie dim green
in broad daylight. The trash keeps coming
and coming in the cold wind and piling
wherever it stops. There are piles and piles of
bottles and cigarette-butts and used condoms,
newspapers and wrappers and liners at every
curbstone, at the foot of each wall.
The whole place stinks of giving-up.

This is where Spider-Man goes when he
wants information about the Green Goblin.
A bar with glowing bottles at the end of the night
where the whole neighborhood gets baby-eyed.
A crowded room of cocky, sullen teens and
grizzled bastards washed up from the
motorcycle street.

My veins are the streets of this city,
my body. Skid Row is my stomach.
A river of bile flows past the brass rail,
the air buckles with jazz,
a cork pops, a green spray of bright notes
dances outta the jukebox, the door
slams, a pin drops,
a dog barks, a glass breaks,

     and day by day
us green-faced fools who live by the river
all fold our plantlike hands and
        pray pray pray in our usual way

CULTURING

T. F. RICE

I am told they
force mussels to birth
pearls
pry their life wide
insert seed
and smile

THE BOY FROM KIEV

TERRY CLARKE

for Aleksey Dayen

1
Kiev to Coney Island
is a long way to go
political refugees
dream in neon, vodka, and snow
see paradise at f.22
hear surf guitars at dawn
Prospero said life's wrapped in sleep
now let the sleepy boy yawn

Chorus
At the end of the life
at the end of the day
my brother the prince
will just slip away
footprints in the sand
from Kiev to Coney Island Avenue

2
Kiev to Coney Island
where flowers die in the trash
ghost radio plays Elvis
the liquor store takes cash
I've got a big guitar
I've got a funeral suit
we'll take the train to nowhere
find where they hid the loot

Chorus

3
Kiev to Coney Island
leather jacket packet of smokes
you fill in the spaces
with what an image evokes
Russian jazz and blues
Irish girl behind the door
you think that you can choose
but truth always wipes the floor

Chorus

LIFE GOES ON

MICHAEL ESTABROOK

We tune in by accident
to the end of *Castaway*,
poor Tom Hanks discovering
that in the four years he has been lost
at sea, stranded on a desolated island,
his beloved wife Kelly has remarried.
"You are the love of my life," she sobs,
holding tightly onto him. But what can she do?
She thought he was dead and has a new life now.

I comment that I wouldn't be able to stand that,
losing my wife, the love of my life, to another man,
no matter what the circumstance.
"Such a sad and terrible thing.
I would be devastated, you know.
I don't think I could bear it," I conclude.

"Oh, come on, life goes on," she states, shrugs,
and pats my shoulder.

WATERWORLD

MICHAEL S. BEGNAL

GLUG-GLUG-GLUG, the rainwater
off the outside of my bldg.,
still voices talking below the open window,

today a film of blue sky remained
behind the swirling dark smoky clouds
which suddenly opened up,
bullets fell in multiple volleys on roof slates,
the cats scurried to their dens in disgust,

with a preponderance of daylight reemerging
I took to the asphalt,
at the bridge I was engulfed

wedged into the right angle of a
rough stone smithy wall/corrugated metal sheet
a tangled branchy mass of ivy hanging overhead,
I wondered what would happen
if I chewed the leaves

stood and imagined the Belgic invasion,
how they came ashore in boats,
waded among the reeds, the marshes, the rushes,
marched along the esker,
built avenues into Turoe
and established their seat

each death finds me in a new location,
a gigantic puddle in the middle of Shop St.,
soon the winter will come,

    r e i n c a r n a t i o n   back on the agenda

THE "WHY" OF ABRAHAM LINCOLN

CEE

Let's not kid ourselves
He was like any Lottery winner
You see those specials
Winners are the saddest, golden breed
Fleshrines of greatness of tears of Nothing godhood
The luckiest
Unlucky people

CROSSROADS

for Bob Kaufman

We met in Tompkins Sq
Late '63 early '64 soon after
J. Kennedy was shot. He followed
Me back to my 5 bucka wk room
Over the Bowery luggage shop where
We could dig Pharoah Sanders
Miles
The horns of R. Kirk
Night after night
Caddycorner over at the 5 Spot.

I had some morphine syringes
Bob had some speed
We sat across the bed shooting drugs
For 2 wks
Jazz pulsating our brains
We wrote
We tore up our poems
We never spoke
Silent screams raging thru
The perpetually undulating factories
Of the mind
Winter cat scratching at the
Steaming windows
War tickling the throats of 2
Continents.

Without a word
We both left the room over the
Luggage shop
We went our separate ways

2 boxes of torn paper
Left at the crossroads
Marked our spot.

HOW TO KILL A FLOWER

SHARON ZEISEL

plant magnolia seeds in rich soil
water responsibly, allow roots to form and drain
flowers should appear full in blossom and in color,
thriving in sunshine.

walk away.

THE BARREL CELLAR (FIRST TEN MINUTES)

M. P. POWERS

In the basement of an old German-style hotel, the waitress
is a candle moving around the tables. Smoke tingles.
Light clings on the brick walls. Night in all
its high forms. She approaches the bar. A potbellied cigarafficionado
with a burning stub shoved between bejeweled fingers,
gazes on her. "Another martini, Marcy."
"Olives?" "Yeah, three. And while you're at it," he says,
"why not drain my balls?" She half-smiles,
blushes. "Better not let Rickey hear that," she says. He flourishes
his cigarhand, takes a drag, takes another and the last.
And then the bald guy beside him
perking up. "I bet she gives some good head," he says.
"Probably got that gag-
reflex down." A couple minutes later, I take a seat
between a Portuguese used-carsalesman and a Ukrainian ex-boxer
who starts telling me all about his craft.
"Vot you do ees you aim fer de cheen ..." he says.
"I don't care who
eet iz. De cheen iz glaas." He stands up, pirouettes
around, swings softly
at the air. The smoke tingling around him. Night in all its high
forms. "De cheen"
he says, "iz glaas. ... I don't care
who eet iz. ..."

IT MAKES NO DIFFERENCE

DAVID SERMERSHEIM

it makes no difference
   if you get up late
   (or not at all)
   can't find your pants
   wear different socks
   miss your bus
   walk in the rain
   lose your way
   come to work
   do nothing but complain

it makes no difference
   no one will know
   who you are
   what you do
   or what you have done
   who or what you know
   (or don't know)

it makes no difference
   what you believe
   think or say
   no one will listen or care
   if you tell the truth or lie
   about what you do
     (alone ... in the dark)

it makes no difference

MY MORNING WALK

PAULA ANNE YUP

for Parker Towle

Not the Appalachian Trail
no blisters like yours
and your grandson
the way you walked this summer
and here in the island fall
nearly Halloween in this warm
Republic of the Marshall Islands
I stroll in my slow sleepiness
until barking nipping dogs
wake me up somewhat
and so I yell at them to stop
while schoolchildren mimic me
yelling stop it and tell me
go to oceanside across the street
and I do and get a coconut on the road
to throw at a little yellow dog
while a family on lagoonside look on
and I guess the palm trees are pretty
and the ocean would astonish
the landlocked person I once was
but you get used to anything
I suppose that is true even with beauty
somewhere near the elementary school
the rain starts so I get drenched
and back in the apartment my plans change
those morning errands will be afternoon
things I must do before physical therapy
and this island has a vote of no confidence
sometime today so I hear and so I read
in the local paper and I'm here typing
doing a load of wash and I already voted
and I guess this is the end to my dry spell
as an absentee American absentee landlady
in this place I call home for this interlude

WE WAIT ALL YEAR FOR THIS

JOHN BERBRICH

And now it's here

Parades, brass bands, fireworks
Glorious snowstorms
Gifts, smiles, big dinners, cakes, candles, songs
A case of wine
A tumbler of schnapps
A keg of imported beer

Oh, look at the children
Laughing, trembling with excitement
Dogs wag tails nonstop
The Super Bowl is on TV
Switch the channel
There's the World Cup
The World Series
Wimbledon
The Masters

I can hardly stand it
Cherry bombs explode across the street
A band marches through our backyard
I'm opening another present
Sucking on a bottle of gin
Working on my taxes
While mailing a love letter to the IRS

Today the whole world is a stadium
A cathedral, a back alley
A street corner where you can get anything
Anything that you want

Here come the fire trucks
Sirens blaring racing down Main Street
Hosing down everyone
Water sprays and sparkles in the sunshine
Turns to ice and glitters

Smile, weep, laugh, pray
It's finally here

PHOTO

ALVIN PARK

I have this image of her
in my head. She is staring
into the camera. She smiles.
She had her hair cut short months
ago, but it's grown out. She
puts it up in a sloppy
bun-slash-ponytail now, which
says more about me than her.
She wears her sunglasses on
top of her head like some
stylish, hip headband. Her bag's
piano-key-patterned strap
hugs the patina of her
red shirt, wraps over her left
shoulder, passes down her chest,
around her right hip, nimbly
disappears. I float atop
a sea of feathering down
blankets, wishing I could live
in that photo with her as
something more than sepia-
toned fingerprint smudges.

KIND TO A SPIDER

TIM STALEY

for Sean Branson, 1977-2004

See, it'll happen like this:
> when I dim the lights
> she'll unhook her safety line
> so I can put her back
> where she's never been.
> My drinking glass
> down around her crown
> as magic carpet slips
> between floor, rim,
> under eight limbs
> until cage and foundation
> are one I levitate,
> sure not to be jiggling
> her red hourglass
> through the living room, and when
> the glass ambulance lifts,
> from the paper stretcher she'll step
> to the perimeter of my property
> and probably, that snake
> won't eat her, and that wind,
> why should it freeze?

And in this way Sean, I wish I'd saved you
and your cat from circling your body for days
until finally she's stuck, whiskers
hard pressed against the window.

LAPSE

in this rare moment of clarity
gerald says
my eyes should be brighter
i should be taller
and more handsome
like he remembers
when we were young

he's right
i stood taller
and my eyes were bright
but i wonder if
he recalls he was taller
and does he know
his eyes are hollow glass now
and not so easy for me to love

i suppose i should be thrilled
he can speak
tho lately he's mistaken me
for my haughty brother
and today he calls me bessie
my long-dead sister's name
just like he used to do
when we dressed
in cowboy garb
to dance the boy bars
and he always said
i wobbled on my boot heels
just like bessie wobbled
on those dreadful pearly stilettos
we bought for her
on our first greyhound outing
from denver
to fredericks of hollywood

then when bessie croaked
her stilettos became sacred
and these days i brush gerald's teeth
the same way i cared for bessie's shoes
but he spits them out
and he gags on baby food
then shakes his fist at me
like he doesn't know who i am

so i shove his dentures
between my own gums
to bite down on bessie's heels
but they pierce my tongue
and i press my face to gerald's breast
just to feel
but the pulse i feel
is my own heart

i'd forsake it all
the days of brighter eyes
the tall
even bessie's heels
for just one moment
of support
from gerald's arms

IT IS WAY TOO EASY TO TAKE EVERYTHING PERSONALLY ...

TIMOTHY BEER

I am slowly slipping in and out of a July sunshine indulgence,
My ineffective mind spacing in the heat.
Overwhelmed
by the floating wave of a wheat field
or the metal-grated fence
figured in
and I tell myself
to count slowly
when the breeze hits

My eyes
flutter between
the monotonous comfort of
my mother in every female animal
and exhaustion.
I
need a creature
to rustle my blood in this dirty afternoon squalor.
I step onto the pavement and I
can feel it in the soles of my shoes.
I stop and I

focus on the skin on my feet.
It feels like the
heat pulling out my face pulling
out my sweat
onto the homeopathic vapor
shining looser than you can

flutter with your compassion.

It's jelled up my brain cells
no fat no water,
it's stopped up my nervous center swaying
in the membranes and I
need a creature to snap me back into place. ...

Ten-pound homeless angel dude tells me to talk to girls.
He asks her what time it is for me,
he did his best—I'm
deciding to respect him instead,
it would be graceful to give my life up to the streets
and the ground and
the god-given natural exception.
... create spirituality in the dirt
and taste it in my lower lip through the harsh
unforgiving afternoon.

COLOPHON

The edition you are holding is the First Print Edition of this complete anthology publication. It comprises five previous issues, published as individual chapbooks without ISBNS, spanning from 2008 to 2012.

Our *Poiesis Review* logo is set in The King & Queen Font, created by Bran, and in Mary Jane Larabie, created by Apostrophic Labs. The interior titles are set in Aruna Vintage, with the author names in Aruna Dirt, both created by Yandi Designs and used with a complete commercial license. The back cover Alternating Current Press logo font is set in Portmanteau, created by JLH Fonts. All other fonts are set in Athelas, created by Veronika Burian and José Scaglione. All fonts are used with permission; all rights reserved.

Front cover artwork: "I Must Get to Boston" by Leah Angstman. The covers of issues no. 1 and 2 were both painted by Leah Angstman. The cover of issue no. 3 was painted by Theo Nelson. The cover of issue no. 4 was painted by Justin Jackley. The cover of issue no. 5 was photographed by Misti Rainwater-Lites. The Alternating Current lightbulb logo was created by Leah Angstman, ©2013, 2020 Alternating Current. The Violet Ray logo was created by Leah Angstman, ©2020 Alternating Current. The photos of T. Kilgore Splake and Robert Schuler were provided by the authors. The Luminaire Award medallions were created by SuA Kang and Devin Byrnes of Hardly Square, hardlysquare.com, for Alternating Current's sole use. All artwork is used with permission; all rights reserved.

The editors wish to thank the font and graphic creators for allowing legal use of their work.

OTHER WORKS FROM
ALTERNATING CURRENT PRESS

All of these books (and more) are available at
Alternating Current's website: press.alternatingcurrentarts.com.

alternatingcurrentarts.com